Sistasflow!
A devotional journey of a broken woman
By Diana Edwards

Sistasflow! Newsletter has been such a blessing to me and countless others. I have been the editor of this newsletter for over four years and God is still giving fresh, invigorating ideas for it. It has and still is encouraging women of all ages. Its distribution has grown tremendously and there are many new subscribers.

I have put together this book of devotionals (some old and some new) that I have written. Some of the content of the previous articles have been slightly changed.

Reflecting back, I realize how life changing these articles have been to me and helped me completely surrender to the Lord. I see the growth I have experienced and it is my hope that others have too.

Sit back, grab a nice cup of coffee, tea or glass of wine; put your feet up and enjoy. My prayer is that these devotionals will continue to equip, empower and encourage you as they did me. Love ya!

Diana Edwards,

Founder, Sistasflow!

Women Unite!

Ecclesiastes chapter 4:9-11

Ladies, it's time for us to come together! The bible says in Ecclesiastes chapter 4 verses 9: *Two are better than one because they have a good return for their labor; if either of them falls down, one can help the other up. But pity anyone who falls and has no one to help him up.* [1]

One major problem that exists between women today is that we don't trust each other. We are afraid of being vulnerable. We are called to be nurturers, not only to our family, but to our friends also. I am almost fifty years old and have had my fair share of drama, but I am grateful to God for the women He has placed in my life. I realized the best way to overcome life's struggles is to be encouraged.

Sistasflow! Ministry is about empowering, equipping and encouraging others to live a life free from oppression; financial burdens; other people's expectations; insecurities; confusion and disorder. In the end, we want to experience freedom; happiness; comfort; security and peace. *We are daughters of the King!*

———————

We live in a fast-paced world, which sometimes strips us of our inheritance. Some of us are depleted physically; spiritually; financially and emotionally. There seems to be nowhere to turn.

But we have a God who loves and cares about us. He will send who we need! He will place women in our lives that will help us focus on our mind, body and spirit!

Women unite!

Crossroads

Acts Chapter 8 & 9

Everyone has had or will have a crossroad experience; a time when choices have to be made. What we do at the crossroad will determine the outcome of our lives.

Have you ever been at a crossroad? A crossroad is a road where one meets another. It is at this intersection, you will have to make a choice of which road to take.

Have you ever taken an unfamiliar road? Regardless of your Mapquest directions or GPS signal, you were still a little unsettled. *What if I miss the next exit? What if I don't see the sign?*

I have traveled unfamiliar roads plenty of times. I would become so anxious about my whereabouts that I would pull into the nearest gas station just to make sure I was on the right road. Without fail, one of two things would happen; I was on the right road or I was lost!

Sometimes we are at a crossroad in our lives. We may have taken a certain road for years and may be led to an unfamiliar one. On this road you may ask, " *What should I do? Should I take this new road or remain on the old one? Is this new road better for my destination? What will I see on this unfamiliar road? Will I see the same things I saw on the other road?*" Pretty scary stuff!

—————————

In the book of Acts, we encounter a man named Saul. He was an over-zealous religious man, who thought his rules and beliefs were the absolute truth. He sought out to kill the *Followers of the Way* (a name they gave followers of Jesus Christ). He went to Damascus to threaten these followers with imprisonment and death. As he walked down a street called Straight, he encountered the one, true living God, Jesus Christ.

Jesus spoke to Saul and challenged him to leave his former life behind and follow him. Saul, astonished and overwhelmed, was blinded at this encounter. After three days, he regained his sight and went on the journey of his life! He became the Apostle Paul, one of history's greatest men.

—————————

We may be at a place where things are just not working anymore. We may be contemplating a career change; answering a call or any other important decision. We may be at a crossroad in our marriages and contemplating divorce. We may be at a crossroad in other significant relationships. We may be at a financial crossroad. We may be like the Apostle Paul, (Saul), blinded by our former passions and beliefs. But I am here to say; maybe it's time for *a change.*

———————

When you encounter a crossroad in your life, don't turn back. It is usually for your own good. You may have to make an unpopular or unfamiliar choice. You may have to relocate, disconnect or reconnect. Don't be disheartened. The Apostle Paul knew in order to follow Christ, he would be ostracized; ridiculed and threatened as he walked into unfamiliar territory, but he did not let that deter his decision at the crossroad. He ultimately took the gospel to the world!

Don't be afraid of the crossroads! You may be used to change the course of history!

What's To Come Is Better than What's Been

Proverbs 23:7

Ladies, we need to adopt this saying: " *You are what you think!* The bible says in Proverbs 23:7: *"For as he thinks in his heart, so is he."* [2] It's time to change our way of thinking!

If we think poverty, we will be poor. If we think failure, we will fail. If we think we will never find love; peace; joy and happiness, we never will. The words we speak have to potential to change our (or others) lives.

———————

What's to come is better than what's been! As women, we have to value our worth. We have so much potential. Take inventory of yourself. It's time to put our gifts; time and talents to use. Step out on faith! If you like to organize trips; parties or dinners, there is a wide market for event planning. If you like to bake or cook, think about catering. If you like to work with children, think about tutoring or opening a day care center. God has placed talents inside of us; we just have to bring them out!

Make a decision that the latter half of your life will be better than the past. Think positive outcomes for your life. Start speaking into your future. Decided not to dwell on the past, but rejoice for your future. Make it a new season! *What's to come is better than what's been!*

Costume Jewelry Verses Diamonds

Read Proverbs 31:10-31

"Who can find a virtuous (excellent, moral character) wife? For her worth is far above rubies?"[3]

I attended a women's conference and one of the speakers gave a perfect analogy of Christian men seeking mates. She was the presenter of a singles workshop and taught on how a "godly" man looks for a mate.

Imagine a man going shopping in a department store looking for a gem. When he approaches the jewelry section, he notices the costume jewelry is out in the open, but the finer jewelry (diamonds) are under lock and key.

This peaks his interest. He wants what's best, so he decides on a diamond. To inquire about a diamond, he has to first get the salesperson's attention to open the case. Then, (only under their watchful eye), will he be allowed to inspect it. After careful inspection, he will make a decision.

There is a huge difference between costume jewelry and diamonds. Costume jewelry is mass produced. Its intention is to try and create the same effect as a real stone. The beads/stones in costume jewelry are reproduced. It looks really nice and may fool some people, but trained eyes know the difference. Wear it awhile and you also will be able to tell the difference.

A diamond comes from the earth. To find a diamond is to find a treasure. Men's lives have been taken over the aspects of diamond hunting.

A diamond has to be cut, polished and then after a long process, the stone must be set. A lot of work goes into a diamond before you see the finished product, but when you do, you will be satisfied.

———————

What about you? How do men see you? Are you costume jewelry or a diamond? In order to become a diamond, you must be willing to let God cut (*take away the negative attitudes*), polish (*take our positive qualities and let them shine*) and set (*place us in the right places and situations*) you?

If we take an introspective look at ourselves, what will we find? Do we exude self-confidence? Do we know who we are? Do we respect ourselves and others? Or are you seen as the proverbial "angry woman"? Do you allow bitterness and resentment to rule in you relationships? Do you respect men? It's time to take a look.

––––––––

God wants to and should be our salesman. Any interested suitors should have to go through Him to get to us. He should be able to tell the interested party our great qualities and what a rare find we are.

Costume jewelry or diamond? What are you seen as? Let God be your salesman! A man should have to go through Him in order to get to you.

People Can't Give You What They Don't Possess

Romans 15:1: We who are strong in faith should help the weak with their weaknesses and not please only ourselves. (NCV)

Recently, I picked up a book by Elder Vikki Johnson, called *Addicted to Counterfeit Love*[4]. She told the story of an encounter with an old acquaintance. She was delighted to see this person, but they didn't return the sentiment. They were cold and standoffish. She tried to engage in small talk, but to no avail. She left disheartened. Then she heard the Lord say: *"People can't give you what they don't possess!"*

Sometimes we tend to set the same standards for friends, family and co-workers, as we set for ourselves. If we feel a person is not responding in the way that we would, we question their judgment. If we give love, we expect love in return. If we are loyal, then we expect loyalty. If we show empathy and compassion, then we expect others to do the same. But what happens when they can't?

If you base your feelings upon what you think a person should do, then you will definitely be disappointed.

There are some people in this world that have never heard a kind word spoken to them. They never had the love and attention of a parent. They have been mistreated by any and every one. This may have caused them to become bitter; critical and unloving.

When we encounter these people, we tend to get upset. We only look at the outside and wonder why they are so ornery. We don't take the time to ask why they act the way they do.

The best thing we can do for them is to accept their shortcomings. Instead of becoming a psychotherapist, trying to figure them out, we need to ask God to heal their broken hearts and souls.

————————

So now when I run into a person who may do things I wouldn't do, I pray for them. My former pastor (and mentor) used to tell me this all the time: "If everyone in the whole world were just like me, what a lovely world it would be!"

When you run into rude, bitter people don't get angry or upset. People can't give you what they don't possess!

Hurricane Season

I love to travel. I love to travel to different countries. I love to cruise. Cruises are very expensive. I had to find a way to cruise to different countries that was cost effective. Then I had a revelation; travel during the months of September, October and November.

For the life of me, I couldn't understand why travel at this time was so cheap. Then one day, a travel agent told me the reason: hurricane season.

————

Hurricane season is a time of uncertainty. Travel plans may be cancelled or evacuations may be encouraged. Itineraries can be turned upside down. These are the consequences for cheaper fare. We may have to weather a storm.

————

Sometimes, we face hurricane seasons in our own lives. It may be sickness or disease; divorce; death; unemployment or anything that would try to blow away our solid foundation.

There can be a warning and we have to decide on our actions. Do we give up or trust God during this season?

Think about an actual hurricane. It is spotted far on the horizon. Meteorologists predict its strength and watches it gain strength as it comes closer inland. If we are in or near its landfall, we may have to make a decision to leave or stay. We may leave or brace ourselves for the worst.

————

When a hurricane makes landfall, it may be tamer or fiercer than predicted. A severe hurricane can bring torrential rains and strong winds. Homes can be uprooted. But after what seems like an eternity, the rain and winds lift and cease. The sun shines as if nothing ever happened.

————

Look at life. Life is full of hurricanes. We may receive a bad report from the doctor and have to make a decision: give up or continue to trust God and fight. We may be going through a divorce and have to make a decision: give up or trust God for emotional healing. We may experience the death of a loved one. Do we give up or allow

God to heal our grief. We may lose our job. Can we trust God for our provision?

————

Just like an actual hurricane, there will be some after effects. There may be things you have to recover (your health; your pride; your finances). There may be a clean-up (a time to let things/people go). There may be a reconstruction period (a time to rebuild your life). This is to be expected. But with the help of a mighty, loving God, we can ride out the hurricane with faith. When the storm comes, get on your knees and pray. Don't give up! It won't last always.

Go through your hurricane season.

Therefore everyone who hears these words of mine and puts them into practice is like a wise man who built his house on the rock. The rain came down, the streams rose and the winds blew and beat against that house; yet it did not fall, because it had its foundation on the rock.[5]

One Rotten Potato

"Do not be yoked together with unbelievers. For what do righteousness and wickedness have in common? Or what fellowship can light have with darkness?"[6]

As I was skimming through a magazine called *The Word of Faith*[7], I ran across a wonderful short story called *One Rotten Potato*. Here is an excerpt:

An eighth grade teacher, wanting to teach her students the effects of offense, asked her students to each bring a bag of potatoes to school for an experiment. They had to empty their bags and each student was given a rotten potato. They were instructed to put the rotten potato at the bottom of the bag. They refilled their bags with the good potatoes and placed it on a shelf. In a few days, the students checked the bags and discovered several of the potatoes surrounding the rotten one, were showing signs of decay. Days later, more potatoes were affected. Before long, the entire bag had decayed. All the potatoes had been affected by one rotten potato!

Have you ever found yourself in that bag of potatoes; in that circle of friends, where one person is always negative, slanderous and bitter? The more you listen to this person, the more their beliefs, attitudes and thought patterns affect your way of thinking. You look at certain things, people and situations differently, once you are in their company. If you share your dreams and passions, they are shot down immediately.

Think about a bag of potatoes. Keeping company with a "rotten potato" can and will affect you. All it takes is one! Look at the people you are keeping company with. Are they lifting you up or dragging you down? How is your spirit around them? Is it at peace or troubled? If your spirit is troubled, leave them alone!

Did you ever see a potato farmer at work? He goes to the field and gathers the potatoes. He carefully inspects each one. He separates the good from the rotten. The good potatoes are prepared for market sale and the rotten ones are discarded.

Don't be like the bag of potatoes. Once you discover a rotten one, get out of its surroundings.

Pleasing God- It's Not What You Think

Hebrews 11:6: But without faith it is impossible to please him; for he that cometh to God must believe that he is, and that he is a rewarder of them that diligently seek him – (KJV)

Man will tell you that the steps to pleasing God are as follows:

1) by attending church every Sunday

2) giving your tithe (ten percent of your salary)

3) and living in perfect harmony with everyone

Sounds great, doesn't it? That's what we want to think.

God says that He is already pleased with you! You are His child! You are loved! He is always with you! You may have missed a Sunday (or ten!), but He still loves you! You may not have enough faith to tithe, but He still loves you! You may not love (or even like) everyone you meet, but He still loves you!

Man will tell you that God is performance-driven, (if you'll do this, then He'll do that!). Man will say that in order to get on God's good side, you must do all the right things all the time and any little slip up will incur His wrath!

God says He loves you unconditionally. He loves with no limits. You can rest! The only person that can separate and deny His love is you!

———————

Pleasing God is very simple; just have faith and acknowledge your relationship with Him. Spend time with Him.

———————

We are His children, and we don't always do the right thing. Think about your own children. Have they disappointed you at one time or another? Did they do things you would rather not talk about? How did you react? Even though they may have displeased you, you still love unconditionally.

We are all prone to make mistakes. God understands that we will probably make more wrong decisions than we can ever imagine. That's doesn't mean He is not pleased with us.

Allow Him to become a part of your life, in the good times and bad. Have faith in Him. Now that would be pleasing to God!

But without faith, it is impossible to please Him!

God Doesn't Make Mistakes

God doesn't *make* mistakes but he does *allow* them! I turned over in my sleep, repeating these words. I woke up wondering what they meant and why I heard them so clearly, so I decided to get deep. I pulled out the dictionary, (as if I didn't know what the word *mistakes* meant!)

The word *mistake* is defined as an: error or fault resulting from defective judgment, deficient knowledge or carelessness.[8] I was taken aback to see the actual meaning of the word. I reflected on the many mistakes made in my life time. I started recalling some decisions, relationships, and opportunities (taken and missed) and acknowledged them for what they were- *mistakes!* I knew the Lord was trying to tell me something.

Maybe He was trying to tell me to stop blaming *Him* (and the devil too!) for some of the things that took place in my life. Maybe He was telling me that a lot of my decisions were made without consulting *Him*, and I should own up to it. Maybe He was telling me that some of the mess I had gotten myself into was because of my own stupidity, carelessness; deficient knowledge... (You fill in the rest).

I want to be transparent here...my marriage was a *mistake*. I should have listened to the Lord before I took that step. He graciously warned me not to get married, but I went ahead anyway. Sadly, it ended in divorce, but the good thing is that God has blessed me with two beautiful sons. God *allowed* this failed marriage in my life. This mistake taught me to love; honor and respect myself and not look for others to do it. This mistake has made me the woman I am today.

In school, whenever I received a test (examination) back, my mistakes were usually circled. The good thing was that the correct answers were in the margin. Given the correct answers, I was able to pass the next test with flying colors!

All things work together for the good to them that love God, to them who are called according to *His* purpose![9] Embrace your mistakes!

Remember, God doesn't make mistakes, but when we do, they can be corrected!

One of the Hardest Pills to Swallow...

...is when you realize you may not matter as much as you thought you did in someone else's life! What do you do when that day comes?

Being a woman of God, the first thing I would suggest is prayer. But what happens when prayer doesn't seem to work? Your heart is breaking. Your pillow is tear-stained. Your mind is ball confusion. What do you do?

If you are like me, you spend hours wondering what went wrong! You question your judgment; analyze your actions; blame stupidity and scream out to God: *WHY*?

I was allowed to visit this place. I saw what certain people really thought about me. I knew that God had sent warnings, but I chose not to heed them. After sifting through the hurt, I was reminded of my selfishness. I saw how badly I wanted to feel loved and accepted. I saw that my loyalty was misplaced. My eyes were opened!

––––––––

I was reminded of the story of Joseph. Joseph had a calling on his life, but he told it (foolishly) to his significant others, his brothers. He bragged that he would be ruler over them and his entire family. He was happy and wanted to share his great news. What did his brothers do when they heard the news? They conspired to kill him.

After being left for dead, sold as a slave and thrown in prison, Joseph was finally promoted. In spite of their evil ways, Joseph showed mercy and forgave his brothers. He understood he had to endure certain things in order to get to the place where God wanted him.

After his promotion, his brothers were afraid of him. He reassured them that he would not retaliate. He told them: *"But as for you, ye thought evil against me; but God meant it unto good.*[10] Their insignificant brother became the greatest influence in their lives!

So, whatever God allows, it will be for your own good. This may be a time of shaking some people loose. This may be a time of getting your priorities in order. This may be a time of reassurance of His love.

God can and will turn it around. He will stop the tears. He will remove the hurt and replace it with peace and joy. *You may seem insignificant to someone else, but to God, you are the apple of His eye!*

Transformed!

One morning, I decided to try a little experiment. Instead of asking God to transform my life, I asked Him to *transform me*. My reasoning was that, maybe if I changed my way of thinking, I would be able to handle this life a little differently.

————

My own little theology of God was warped. I saw God as a *genie* (someone who could make my debts magically disappear); a *soothsayer* (someone who could make a man love or like me); a *terminator* (someone who could get rid of my problems); a *personal financier* (someone who could get me a new house; new car and more money) and a *movie director* (someone who would call cut and start a new take).

After this little experiment, I saw God for who He really was! He was my *Savior;* someone who was able to keep me from falling and present me without fault.[11] Plain and simple!

So instead of looking for a *genie,* I took authority over my debt and moved on. Instead of jumping through hoops to get someone to love me, I started loving myself. Instead of wishing for someone to purchase material things, I decided to save money and go after them myself.

———————

My will is not my own and before I take on any new adventure, I find out what God thinks about it. My mind has been totally transformed!

Ask the Lord to transform your mind

I AM...

Who God says I am! I am:

1. *Victorious* – *1 Corinthians 15:57:* But thanks be to God, who gives us victory through our Lord Jesus Christ

2. *Precious* – *Isaiah 43:4:* Since you were precious in my sight, you have been honored and I have loved you.

3. *Wonderfully made* – *Psalm 139:14:* For I am fearfully and wonderfully made

4. *A heir and child of God* – *Romans 8:16:* The Spirit bears witness with our spirit that we are children of God and if children, then heirs – heirs of God and joint heirs with Christ

5. *Protected* – *Psalm 91:1:* He who dwells in the secret place of the Most High, shall abide under the shadow of the Almighty.

I believe I am what God says I am!

If God says we have victory through Christ Jesus, then why won't we acknowledge Him in our choices, decisions and actions? If God says we are precious, then why do we allow others to make us feel worthless and not valued? If God says we are wonderfully made, then why do we compare ourselves with others? If God says we are His children and heirs, they why do we allow people to treat us like stepchildren? If God says we're protected, then why do we live out our lives in fear?

––––––––

I have spoken to many women who feel they don't deserve better than what they have. Hidden guilt and shame dictates their lives. There are women who have been abused (both physically and emotionally) and are ashamed to tell their story. There are single mothers who are bearing the brunt of responsibility, ashamed or scared to ask for help. There are women in relationships, shouldering all of the financial burdens. There are women who are allowing their children to dictate and run their lives. There are angry women, who allow their resentment and bitterness spill over into their everyday lives. *WHY?*

Moses asked God who he would say has sent him. He told him to tell them I AM sent you.

Let's make a vow today. Remember who is with you, I AM. Let's write these scriptures on a piece of paper and place them everywhere you can think of. Put these truths on the bathroom and bedroom mirror, so that every time you look at yourself, you see who you are! Start believing the Lord!

I AM what God says I AM!

Let God Handle the Results

Most of us have prayed and asked the Lord to fulfill, bless, give and allow certain things to happen in our lives. We pray with expectation. We expect God to do things exactly the way we want it. *But what happens if He doesn't?* What happens when God decides that job; man; house or position is not for you? What happens if that bundle of joy never arrives? What happens if that loved one dies? What happens if the man of your dreams walks out on you? What happens when God's results are not what we expected?

———————

I have been in this situation numerous times. I prayed, telling God what I wanted, only to be disappointed. My prayers were actually thinly veiled demands. I knew what was best for me, so I told God what I wanted to happen.

When things didn't turn out how I expected them to, I was disappointed, heartbroken and frustrated. I didn't understand or accept that God knew what was best for me. I found myself becoming angry at Him. It became a vicious cycle of demands and frustration.

––––––––––

One Sunday, while worshipping in church, I felt different. I humbly told the Lord that I was "tired of fighting Him." I didn't want to be in control anymore. I was tired of seeing the same old results to the same old prayers. So what did I do? I gave up all of my ideas; plans; ministries; relationships; desires (and anything else I could think of) and handed them over. I let God take charge. The results are in *His* hands.

––––––––––

Sisters, if the results of your prayers are not what you anticipated; it may be the Lord rearranging, reorganizing and restructuring some things. Take it as a blessing.

Give God the problem, He will handle the results!

Life Unexpected

What happens when life throws you a "curve ball"? Death; sickness; divorce; unemployment and tragedy can strike at any time. Who do you turn to?

Recently, I have received phones calls stating: *my brother was hospitalized with a stroke; my cousin suffered two near fatal brain aneurysms; a good friend was been diagnosed with terminal cancer; a co-worker suffered a heart attack and another suffered a brain aneurysm and passed away.* Life unexpected!

———

What do you say to people about unexpected trials? What do you say to the sufferer or their loved ones? Do you remind them of God's goodness during the time of storms? Do you tell them you are praying for them? Do you remain silent?

What do you say to a person who was told by their doctors, they only had a few months to live?

I was placed in this situation. At first I was at a loss for words, and then I immediately prayed for wisdom. I reassured him that Jesus loved him and that He would be with him, in spite of the outcome. I told him to look to Christ for comfort and strength. I empathized with him, but truthfully told him that I didn't (and couldn't possibly) understand how he felt. I told him that he could count on me being there for him.

Being a Christian doesn't exempt you from life. There will be heartache; disappointment and tragedy. What we must do is to dig deeper in Jesus. When life is good, we get complacent. We assume that everything will continue to go well. We may even think we don't need the Lord anymore. Nothing can be further from the truth!

Jesus saved us from a life of sin. He doesn't guarantee there will be no trouble, but He does guarantee eternal life.

So to my brother; cousin; friend; co-workers (and their families), Jesus cares! He is there for you. The end result may not be what we expect, but you can hold to *His* hand when life is unexpected!

When life is unexpected, hold to His hand, God's unchanging hand!

A Kept Woman

What normally comes to mind when you hear a "kept woman"? Usually it means a woman who is involved in a long term extra-marital affair. She is usually well-hidden (from the wife) and well protected. Her suitor will make sure she maintains a comfortable (and sometimes, lavish) lifestyle. The man falls head over heels in love with her and will do anything not to lose the relationship (regardless of his marital status). To sum it up: a kept woman is someone who is *shielded; provided for; protected and loved.*

I am not by any means advocating adultery! I want you to look at this term in another light. *What does it mean to be kept by God?*

Once a relationship with God has been established, He will pursue you. He will touch your heart. He becomes a major part of your life. He loves you and will make you *the apple of His eye.* [12] He makes sure you are well hidden and will cover you. [13]

He will protect you. [14] He is a provider. [15] He will help you maintain your lifestyle. [16] You are His! [17]

———————

There is a purpose for being kept by God; to allow the best to come into your life. God has special plans for you. He only wants what's best. He knows about the people you are in relationship with. He knows what man will love you unconditionally and which will break your heart. He knows what man will provide a good life for you. He wants to keep you from hurt, harm and danger. God looks at the heart. Let Him keep you until He's ready...

I want to be a kept woman!

Defeated Lives

The living God says He is our: Father; provider; protector; healer and friend. If this is true, then why as, His children, do we live defeated lives?

After studying the Old Testament, I discovered God. To the Israelites, He was a provider. To King David, He was a protector. To King Hezekiah, He was a healer. To Abraham, He was a friend.

In the New Testament, I saw Jesus Christ heal blind Bartimaeus, raise Lazarus from the dead; feed the multitudes and go to Calvary for our sins.

If the Lord did all of this for these people, why can't He do it for me?

———————

In this life, we may have to combat serious issues and circumstances. There is poverty; strife; sickness; disease; divorce; infidelity and the list goes on. When trouble comes, we usually ask the Lord to take it away. Sometimes, He does and sometimes He does not. This is when doubt and defeat arise.

Once I prayed for God to take something that I perceived as a problem away from me. Then one day, a thought popped into my head. I was asking for the wrong thing! I suddenly asked God to give me the strength to go through this dilemma. Immediately I felt the burden lift. I realized that if God is who I say He is, He will minister and provide for me, whatever the outcome. He will give me the wisdom and the strength that I need. After all, He is God!

———————

God knows and cares all about you. He wants you to win. If you need strength to go through a particular situation, ask Him. The problem may not change, but I am certain you will.

God is the greatest power, we won't be defeated!

Are You Really Ready For Your Blessing?

In Matthew 25, Jesus shares a parable (story) about ten virgins who went out to meet the bridegroom. Five were wise and five were foolish. The wise women trimmed their lamps with oil. The foolish women didn't put any oil in their lamps, so they had to run out and buy some. While they were away, the bridegroom arrived. *Guess who wasn't ready to go into the wedding?*

Recently, I had a strange dream. I dreamt that I had just given birth to a baby boy and was ecstatic! After settling down, I realized I didn't prepare for this birth and had nothing to take care of this baby. Frantic, I ran to the store searching for bottles, diapers and clothing. There was none. Heartbroken, I turned around and explained to another customer what had happened. I told her that I knew my child was a blessing from God, but I wasn't ready for it!

After waking up from this dream, I kept asking myself if I was ready for God's blessings in my life. This was strange because I consider myself as someone who is prepared for everything.

At that moment, I knew that God was trying to tell me something. If He were to bless me abundantly, would I be able to handle it? Would I be ready to receive it? Am I prepared?

———————

Most of us are praying for specific things. We may be praying for husbands, a higher paying job, a new house or physical healing. If God would decide to bless you at this very moment, would you be ready?

Those of you praying for that perfect mate; are you that perfect mate? If God were to bless you right now, are you ready?

For those of you praying for that higher paying job; are you willing to accept the sacrifices you may have to make?

For those of you praying for that new house, car or any other material thing; are your finances in order?

———————

As children of God, He wants to bless us tremendously, but if we are not prepared, it could turn into a disaster. This means we must be willing to work on our attitudes; our willingness; our finances; our health and anything that would get us ready to receive God's best. We need to be ready at all costs.

———————

The smart virgins had their lamps trimmed with oil and waited patiently for the bridegroom to appear. The foolish felt they had time to prepare and was left out at the time of blessing. Are you ready for what God wants to give you?

Be ready for your blessing!

Being Alone vs. Being Lonely

Someone once said: *"Being alone helps you build a healthy relationship with yourself; being lonely helps you build unhealthy relationships with others."* Oh how true!

———————

Being alone is different from being lonely. You may be thrust into situations that can cause you to be alone, but how you react to it will define whether you are alone or lonely.

When you are alone, be it from singleness; divorce; an "empty nest", etc., you can enjoy this period in your life. You can take this time to get to know yourself a little better. You can take this time to understand what makes you *tick*. You can look at past mistakes and decide to move one. You can build your relationship with the Lord and start loving yourself.

When you are lonely, you tend to depend upon others to make you feel better about yourself. You may subject yourself to certain people and situations that are not healthy for you. You may frequent places that may not be right for you. You wind up settling for less than what God has for you!

I have been in a "lonely" state. I have placed myself in ungodly relationships because I was lonely. I did desperate things because I was lonely. I threw caution to the wind and wound up with being manipulated and controlled.

Here is a funny story that I often share. In my "lonely" state, I dated a man that I knew was wrong from the start. I fell hard for this man. After much heartache and drama, God had graciously removed him from my life. A few years later, I had run into him and we started reminiscing about the good times. He heard I had gone to seminary and was impressed. After small talk, we decided to go out to dinner (and whatever else!).

Usually I would pray about dates, but I knew this was wrong, (and I knew God's answer) so I didn't bother. I went about preparing myself for my date. Twenty minutes before the agreed upon time, I received a phone call from my "date", saying that *he* didn't think it was a good idea. He told me that he knew that I was getting my life right and didn't want to interfere. *Talk about God intervening!* I hung up the phone speechless!

I knew the only reason I agreed to go out with him was because of loneliness. I am sure I would have wreaked havoc in both of our lives if God had not intervened.

I learned to look at my state of singleness as being alone verses being lonely. Being alone has changed my relationship with me and (best of all), with God. You will never be lonely if you love the Lord. He will never leave or forsake you!

Give God your loneliness and get to know yourself better. I did and found a good woman, mother, daughter, friend, acquaintance and co-worker, waiting: me!

Being alone introduced me to someone new: me!

Relax!

Colossians 3:15: Let the peace of Christ rule in your hearts, since as members of one body you were called to peace and be thankful[18]

We all need to relax; not learn how to relax; not think about relaxing; not plan to relax, just relax!

I woke up in the middle of the night and felt strange. My mind was blank! I didn't think about anything! I wasn't worried about anything! This was strange and unfamiliar territory for me. I was a little frightened. I tried to conjure up my problems, but couldn't. I tried to bring all of my worries and issues to my mind, but couldn't. I didn't understand what was happening.

Since I am rarely in this state, I didn't know what to do. I pondered on whether to continue to try and rehash my worries to feel comfortable or should I just relax, turn over and go back to sleep? I chose the latter.

———

Some of us have been robbed of our peace for many years. We don't know what it means to relax and let go.

We feel we must be proactive and handle every issue or everything that comes our way.

We analyze every comment made to us and analyze every conversation we engage in. Somehow, we mystically *know* what others are thinking and psychoanalyze their thought patterns.

When we feel something is not right, we pull out all resources and try to fix it. We press the rewind button and replay every unpleasant circumstance or situation in our minds over and over again.

We take the weight of other people's worlds on our shoulders. We fear what they think, making us afraid to say no to their demands.

We must relax and let go!

To relax means to make lax or loose (as in a grip); to reduce in intensity; to relieve from strain or to become less severe or strict[19]

This means we may have to loosen our hold on our spouse; significant other; children or whomever we have a firm grip on. We need to stop being so intense and look for the simplest solution or answer to the problem first.

If we are in strained relationships, we may need to take a break-even if it's for one hour. Go for a walk and smell the flowers. Lastly, we must stop being so hard on ourselves. Things happen; they will happen and are going to happen again and again. This is part of life. Once we can take a hold of this nugget, we can relax and not worry.

Pray that God will teach you how to relax. And remember to be thankful!

Destiny

I once heard a bishop say: "Sometimes God has to include the plan of the enemy in order to push you to your destiny!

Destiny. What exactly does that mean? It is defined as a pre-determined course of events considered as something beyond human power of control. [20]

This word means nothing when you have experienced unmitigated pain in your life. It means nothing when *hell-hounds* are on your trail. It means nothing when you think of the mental or physical abuse you may have been subjected to. Who wants to think about destiny?

The bible tells a story about a man with a destiny. [21] David was shepherd boy and a man after God's own heart

God had His hand upon David. He set him up to replace King Saul. From the time of his first anointing, it became a long and difficult journey, full of accusations and death threats. It was a journey one should not have to take.

David became a fugitive; lived in a cave and had a price put on his head. King Saul wanted him dead. In the natural eye, that should have been the end of him, but God saw differently. He orchestrated a plot to take the kingdom away from Saul and give it to the destined king, David. He became ruler over God's people. This did not happen overnight. It took years for David to meet with his destiny.

———————

What about you? What has or is stopping you from fulfilling your destiny? Is it an abusive childhood? Were you abandoned by those that should have loved you? Were you neglected by your parents? Did you feel unloved? Were you raised in poverty with drug-addicted or alcoholic parents? The list can go on and on. It's time to stop letting your past dictate your future.

Take a look at your past and where you are now. In spite of everything, God has kept you and wants to fulfill His plans for your life.

Grab a hold of your destiny and never let go!

You are destined for greatness. Allow your hurts to be the salve for other's wounds.

True Forgiveness

True forgiveness is giving up the right to hurt the person that has hurt you – Anonymous

For most of my life, I had a silent killer living with me. It was slowly robbing me of my physical and emotional health. Stress, high blood pressure and depression were some of its ammunition.

This killer was tricky. It would resurface at the most inopportune times. It lurked around, interrupting conversations. It would barge in at joyous occasions. It became the center attraction in many of my relationships. Who (or what) is this silent killer? It goes by the name of unforgiveness.

Unforgiveness will make you rehash old hurts. It will make you moody and unstable. It will make you a hypocrite. It will isolate you. It will make you do and say things that are hurtful to others. It will magnify your fears and cause you to feel rejected. It takes over your life.

The first step to letting go of unforgiveness is to give up the right to hurt the person that hurt you. There may have been devastating circumstances, but God says that vengeance is His. He knows what took place and He will deal with the problem.

We cannot allow the enemy to steal our joy any more. Yes, people can and will hurt you, but we must not allow them to have power over our lives. You may ask what power they have. They have the power to control our every thought and action; the power to allow us to make decisions based on their actions. We might not frequent a particular place or go to a function, afraid that we will run into them. We can't listen to a particular song or watch a certain movie because of the painful memories. They are probably not even aware of the power they hold. They are going on with life as normal.

———————————

Let's stop seeking vengeance and give them back their power. Ask God to help you forgive them and yourself. Let it go.

If they aren't suffering any repercussions from their behavior towards you, thank God for His mercy and move on! This is true forgiveness!

Unforgiveness can block God from answering your prayers! Let it go!

Epilogue

These devotionals are an attempt to show others how God has worked in my life. I am still a work in progress and am excited to see what God will do in the future. Reading these words has bought tears to my eyes, seeing how bound and oppressed I really was. God needed me to surrender everything unto Him and years later, I can truly say that I have! I am letting God take control.

It is my hope people will read some of these entries and apply them to their own lives. It is my prayer that everyone finds a deeper relationship with the Lord. He loves us all.

Diana Edwards

A Simple Prayer

If you never had a relationship with Jesus Christ and want one, here are some simple steps:

1.   Admit that you are a sinner

2.   Be willing to repent (turn from sin)

3.   Believe that Jesus Christ died for you and rose again

4.   Invite Jesus into your heart to be your Savior

Here is a simple prayer:

"Dear God, I know that I am a sinner and believe you died on the cross for me. Please wash me from all sin and come into my life as Lord and Savior. I ask this in your name Jesus, Amen!"

It is done! Welcome my sister!

Footnotes:

---

[1] New International version

[2] Amplified Bible

[3] Proverbs 31:10 – New King James version

[4] 2007, Kimani Press

[5] Matthew 7:24 – New International Version

[6] 2 Corinthians 6:14 – New International version

[7] Kenneth Hagin Jr. Ministries – November 2008 issue

[8] American Heritage Dictionary

[9] Romans 8:28

[10] Genesis 50:20 – King James Version

[11] Jude 24: Kings James version (paraphrased)

[12] Psalm 17:8 – Keep me as the apple of your eye

[13] Exodus 17:15 – The Lord is our Banner (Jehovah Nissi)

[14] Psalm 91:10 – "No evil shall befall you"

[15] Genesis 22:14 – "The Lord will provide" (Jehovah Jireh)

[16] Matthey 6:31 – "There do not worry what you will eat or drink or wear" (paraphrased)

[17] Exodus 19:5 – "For you are my treasured possession"

[18] New International version

[19] The Freedictionary.com

[20] The Free Dictionary.com

[21] Read 1 Samuel 15 – 2 Samuel 5